When Is Christ Being Seen in Us?

Second Edition

By John E. Best, Th.D.

When Is Christ Being Seen in Us?
Unless otherwise noted, the material in this study has been produced by John E. Best.
© 2009 First Edition John E. Best
© 2010 Second Edition John E. Best

You may only copy portions of the material herein with the following stipulations:
a. That credit is given to John E. Best. The publishers and website should be included as well as the copyright notice.
b. That you not copy the portions that others have copyrighted. You must get permission to copy it for your purposes from the original publisher or author.
c. That you not copyright any of this material yourself. We want to be free to publish this material.
d. You may use brief quotations in reviews and a few (less than 5) pages for personal or group study. This is encouraged and will be permitted. Please contact the publisher for permission.
e. Copying and reproducing for personal or commercial gain or profit will not be permitted.

Please note that the publishers, not the author, should be contacted for permission or other matters

Unless otherwise indicated, the Scripture quotations in this publication are from the New American Standard Bible, Copyright © 1960, 1962, 1963, 1968, 1971, 1972, 1973, 1975, 1977, 1995 by the Lockman Foundation. Used by permission. (www.Lockman.org)

Cover Art: miblart.com

Abundant Living Resources

A label of
Grace Fellowship International
www.GraceFellowshipInternational.com

Providing the needed truth of the grace of God, found in union with the life of Christ in His cross and His indwelling.

TABLE OF CONTENTS

Dedication 5

Prologue: What is the Exchanged Life? 7

Introduction: The Problem 11

When Is Christ Being Displayed in Us? 25

The Character of Christ: First Chart 33

The Character of Christ: Second Chart 49

Scriptures about Love 65

Testimonies 67

Bibliography 85

Cited Authors 101

Dedication

To **Donna Corb**
Brannin McNeill
David Quine
Diana Sollars

I meet with these four people, whom I call "the ministers of multiplication," every month or so and they give me feedback. They have critiqued the earlier drafts of my newer books such as this one. Their suggestions have been valuable to me and have resulted in this and my other books being better than they'd be otherwise.

Three of them were my students in the Advanced Teaching and Training of Exchanged Life Ministries Texas. My connection with them has continued and has developed into them now being dear friends and loving servants of Christ with me.

Prologue:
WHAT IS THE EXCHANGED LIFE?

At the moment of our salvation, God exchanged our old identity as **sinners** in Adam for a radically new identity in Christ. We are now not just sinners saved by grace; our essential nature and identity is that of new creation **saints** in Christ. God did this by making our union with Christ so real, so vital, so complete, and so trans-historical that the old us (our spirit) in Adam died at the cross and was buried with Christ. The new us (our spiritual identity) is now raised up in union with Him. We have been set free to live as ones who have been made brand new in Christ's resurrection (Romans 6). This is God's doing. He traded our old identity in Adam for a new identity in Christ.

This is the *FOUNDATION* of the **exchanged life**: God's uniting us with Christ, whose life is eternal. This results in a **shared life**, a life of union with Christ. We are "in Christ" and He is "in us" (Galatians

2:20; John 14:20). We can then experience intimacy with God.

However, the usual experience for us as Christians seems to be that we lose sight of our resources in Christ. The great tendency is for us to want our own way, to try to get our needs met our way and to depend upon our own human resources (the flesh) instead of upon Him. Even the Apostle Paul described his own personal struggle and defeat as he strove in his own strength to fulfill the will of God (Romans 7:14-25).

We need to be brought to a place like Paul where we give up on our fleshly efforts and turn from all attitudes of independence, because by these we deny the fact of our union, our shared life in Christ (John 7:37-39; 15:1-11; Romans 15:18; 2 Corinthians 3:5-6; Galatians 2:20; Philippians 1:20-21; 3:1-13). This is the APPROPRIATION of the **exchanged life.**

To experience what God has provided us in the exchanged life and to walk in victory over the power of indwelling sin (Romans 6:1-14), we must continue to **trust resolutely** in what the Bible says about our union with Christ in His death, burial, resurrection and ascension and His powerful presence within. As we continue to appropriate His life rather than relying on ourselves, Christ meets our inner needs and gives us His joy, peace, power and a deeper walk with Him in the midst of life's difficulties and problems. The focus of our attention is shifted from ourselves to Christ and those He has put into our lives for Him to love through us (John 15:9-17; 1 Corinthians 13; Galatians 5:13-18; 1 John 3:16–4:12). As Christ lives His life through us, He will be seen in us (Galatians 2:20; Philippians 1:20-21).

This is the *RESULT* of the **exchanged life.** By an ongoing trust in Christ as our life, we can trade our total insufficiency to live the life the New Testament describes for Christ's total sufficiency to live it in and through us. As Richard Hall states:

> "*The exchanged life is the exchange
> (with Christ at the cross)*
> **of**
>
> **a self-centered life lived out of the Christian's own resources as if he were still in Adam,**
>
> **for**
>
> **a Christ-centered life lived out of Christ's resources because he is in Christ.**"

Introduction
THE PROBLEM

For a long time I wondered, "If Christ is my life,[1] how will I know if He is being seen in me?" This is an important question because Scripture says that Jesus Christ desires to live His life in and through us.[2] But how would I know if He is being seen through me?

If I am depending upon my *feelings* to answer this, I will be on an internal roller coaster. During a praise time at church, it may seem that Jesus is being seen (or heard) through me. But when I'm tired in the morning, when someone "puts me down," or when my prayers are not answered the way I hoped they would be, I will doubt, based upon my feelings, that He is being seen through me. Could it be that my flesh is connecting to my negative feelings to bring this waffling to the surface?

---

1 Colossians 3:4. See also the Prologue, "What is the Exchanged Life?"

2 Romans 15:13; 2 Corinthians 2:14; Galatians 2:20; Philippians 1:20-21.

If I'm trying to prove by my feverish *activity* that Christ is being displayed through me, I may think He is being seen if these are "Christian" activities. However, what happens when I have to go to work at a "secular" job or worse yet, I am so sick I can't do anything? Is there a way, apart from emotions and commotion, that I can know for sure that Christ is being seen in and through me?

If you live or work with someone who is critical of you, someone who is hard to live with, the question is more acute. When they belittle, discount, accuse and condemn you, it is natural to wonder if Christ is being seen in you!

Or perhaps the criticism of you comes not from *without*; rather, it comes from *within*. If you have a sensitive or guilty conscience and a tendency to be critical of yourself, this question about Christ being seen in you may be frustrating and painful. Do you accept this criticism from without or from within?

Do you see yourself as frequently failing in the Christian life in spite of your assiduous and unfailing trust in Christ? If you do, is this a productive perception of your personhood? Could it be that your focus is more on yourself than Christ?[3] How will you know if it is?

---

3   If you do have a predilection to be critical of yourself, remember that Paul, the one who could put the most confidence in his flesh (Philippians 3:3-9), said that on the other hand all of his adequacy came from God (2 Corinthians 3:5-6).

What will Christ living through you look like? When is Christ being seen in you? Could there be a way to answer these questions that will be both encouraging and empowering[4] to us and glorifying to God?[5] That's what this book will answer.

My Proposal

When the Lord led me to His answers to these perplexing problems, I could finally relax. I could trust that Christ was being expressed in me whether I thought or felt that He was![6] Here is what I discovered and what I propose as the answer to your dilemma in this matter:

> **Christ is being seen in my life when His character is being displayed in me.**

---

4   Philippians 4:13, "I can do all things through Christ, who strengthens me."

5   Philippians 1:20-21.

6   "One of the most significant things that God has done is given me a deepened and renewed trust in Christ's adequacy to be truly responsible for me and all related to me. This is in stark contrast to the weight of responsibility that I have often felt... Can you imagine the stress that ... performance based acceptance put on me? It was such a relief to find release from this stress in Christ! God spells relief, J E S U S." John E. Best, ***Exchanged Lives*** (Garland, TX: Abundant Living Resources, 2002), pp. 43-44. www.AbundanLivingResources.org.

Picture the people of Jesus' time crowded around Him. See them observing not only His outer appearance but also His inner character.[7] The apostle John aptly called the Lord Jesus Christ, "the Word" (Greek, *Logos*). In doing so in John 1:1-18, he asserted that He "was the Shekinah Glory in open manifestation, ... the personal manifestation, not of part of the Divine nature, but of the whole Deity."[8] "And the Word became flesh and dwelt among us and we beheld His glory, glory as of the only begotten from the Father, full of grace and truth" (John 1:14).

We today can also read about this character of Christ in His life on earth. We have much biblical data on this.[9] But this is a lot of material to keep

---

[7] Rather than our asking ourselves, "What would Jesus do?" or better, "What would Jesus want me to do?" there is a better question, "Am I living in such a dynamic union with Jesus that He is producing His character in me?" Put more simply, "Lord, am I trusting you to live your life in me? May the beauty of Jesus be seen in me."

[8] W. E. Vine, *The Expanded Vine's Expository Dictionary of New Testament Words* (Minneapolis: Bethany House Publisher, 1984), p. 1242.

[9] Matthew, Mark, Luke, and John have 89 chapters. Innumerable volumes have been written by Bible scholars. For instance, Alfred Edersheim, *The Life and Times of Jesus the Messiah* (New York: Longmans, Green, 1912), 2 volumes; John Peter Lange, *The Life of the Lord Jesus* (Grand Rapids: Zondervan Publishing House, translated 1958), 4 volumes; J. Dwight Pentecost, *The Words and Works of Jesus Christ* (Grand Rapids: Zondervan Publishing House, 1981), 629 pages; W. Graham Scroggie, *A Guide to the Gospels* (London: Pickering & Inglis Ltd., 1948), 663 pages. As Scroggie shows, much of the Gospels focus on the Cross. Pp. 547-48.

in mind to see if His character is being displayed in us. Can His character be summarized or epitomized in some way?

It was fascinating to me to discover that some of the chief characteristics of Christ's character are found in the fruit of the Spirit (Galatians 5:22-23) and in the facets of godly, *agapē* love (1 Corinthians 13:4-8). I will show this later and cite many examples from Christ's life.

To repeat this liberating and relaxing principle: **I can know that Christ is being seen in my life when His character is being displayed in me.** This will look like the character of Christ on earth, the fruit of the Spirit and the aspects of *agapē*![10] Learning about this and letting Christ live His life in and through you can lead you to rest in your Christian life as it did me.

---

10 However, I wish to make it crystal clear that there are many attributes and actions of Jesus that will not, indeed, cannot be produced in us. C. S. Lewis explained one of them:

"We can all understand how a man forgives offenses against himself. You tread on my toes and I forgive you, you steal my money and I forgive you. But what should we make of a man, himself unrobbed and untrodden on, who announced that he forgave you for treading on other men's toes and stealing other men's money? Asinine fatuity is the kindest description we should give of his conduct. Yet this is what Jesus did." ***Mere Christianity*** (San Francisco: Harper Collins Publishers, 1952, 2001) p. 51.

Why This Wording?

It is necessary to see more about the actual question proposed before I develop the proof of the answer.

The question was: when is Christ being seen in me? The question was not:

- How will I know when Christ is living His life through me?
- How will I know when others are walking by faith?
- How can I strive to have Christ live His life in me?
- How can I focus on being more Christ-like?

Let's take these four questions one by one and see why I'm not asking them.

How will I know when Christ is living His life in me?

The answer to this is simple: I know it by faith. If I've given up on my flesh to try to live the Christian life, and if I have seen that only Christ can live it through me, and if I have asked Him to do so, *why would He **not** do it?*

He wants to reproduce His life in me more than I want Him to; so since I've asked Him to do so, why wouldn't He do just that?[11]

So I should not look to Christ's character (in His earthly life or fruit of the Spirit or *agapē* love) to prove that He is living His life in me. I should only ask, "Am I trusting Him to do so?"[12] If the answer is "yes," then I am walking by faith and this is what pleases Him.[13]

Looking for Christ's character qualities has one purpose: to see if He is being reflected in me to **others**. It is so vital that He be reflected to onlookers! Hannah Whitall Smith cautions us:

> A complaining Christian, an exacting Christian, a selfish Christian, a cruel, hardhearted Christian, a self-indulgent Christian, a Christian with a sharp tongue or bitter spirit, may be a very earnest worker and

---

11 Especially see on this Bill Gillham, **Lifetime Guarantee** (Eugene, OR: Harvest House Publishers, 1987, 1993) pp. 165-71. Or Bill Gillham, **The Life** Video Series (Stafford, TX: Mars Hill Productions and Ft. Worth, TX: Lifetime Guarantee Ministries, Inc., 1996), session 8a.

12 Do not ask, "*How much* am I trusting Him?" as if you needed a greater quantity of faith. See Bill Gillham, **What God Wishes Christians Knew about Christianity** (Eugene, OR: Harvest House Publishers, 1998), chapter 12. "God Wishes Christians Knew that They Have All the Faith They Need."

13 2 Corinthians 5:7; Hebrews 11:6.

have an honorable place in the Church, but, he or she is *not* a Christlike Christian... We must, in short, be real followers of Christ, not followers in theory only.[14]

When Jesus walked this earth He was the perfect God-man ontologically, just by Who He was, whether He did anything to show it or not. However, as He lived He **showed** that He was the Son of God and Son of Man. His character qualities did not make Him Who He was, they **demonstrated** it to others.[15]

Likewise, Christ is Who He is within us by the fact of His being. We know that by faith.[16] He is reproduced in us and *seen by others* as He displays His character through us.[17]

---

14 Hannah Whitall Smith, ***The Christian's Secret of a Happy Life*** (New Kensington, PA: Whitaker House, 1983), p. 188.

15 Jesus said, "... The works which the Father has given to me to finish – the very works I do – bear witness for me, that the Father has sent me" (John 5:36). His disciples concluded "now we are sure that you know all things ... by this we believe that you came forth from God" (John 16:30).

16 Galatians 2:20b "... I live by faith in the Son of God ... ."

17 Philippians 1:20-21.

How will I know when others are walking by faith?

I have not proposed this question because our flesh has a great tendency to be critical of others. The enemy wants to get our focus off Christ onto **anything** else away from Christ.[18] Satan will, through the power of indwelling sin, tempt our flesh to examine how other Christians are doing.[19] God has called us to abide in Christ **ourselves** and be, through Him, fruit *bearers*, not fruit *inspectors*.[20]

How can I strive to have Christ live His life in me?

I have not asked this question because answering it results in a conundrum, an unsolvable puzzle. For if Christ is to live His life, and if this is a life of rest,[21]

---

18 This propensity to examine others can be seen in those who emphasize that works must immediately follow salvation or one is not saved. However, it is not just thoroughgoing Reformed theologians who spend time and attention on this. It is a tendency of all of us.

19 "Who are you to judge the servant of another? To his own master he stands or falls; and stand he will, for the Lord is able to make him stand" (Romans 14:4).

20 I am well aware of the current controversy over "Lordship salvation," but a discussion of it is not within the scope of the topic.

21 Hebrews 3 and 4 declares that it is by faith that God's rest is entered (See especially 3:19; 4:2).

how could it be entered by our striving?[22] So striving and struggling will not produce this supernatural life. Trying to imitate Christ's character qualities, or the fruit of the Spirit, or the aspects of *agapē* will only lead to frustration and unrest. David Needham says it well: "God has not asked us to exchange one kind of stress – the stress of the world – for another kind – the stress of holiness."[23] Someone else has said that if we work to get out of the work system (being under Law), we will find that it does not work! This is hardly the easy yoke and the light burden that Christ promised.[24]

Yet I labored under this yoke and burden for a long time. After 37 years of this I saw that I would never be able, even by my most earnest and best efforts to emulate Christ's character, the fruit of the Spirit, or the aspects of *agapē* love.[25]

So I am going to show later the correlation between the three facets of Christ's reflection through us (the

---

[22] It is true that Paul spoke of laboring and striving in the ministry in Colossians 1:29, but he was quick to add that he did this "... according to His power, which mightily works within me." See also Steve McVey, **Grace Amazing** (Eugene, OR: Harvest House Publishers, 2001), pp. 96-97.

[23] David Needham, **Birthright** (Sisters, OR: Multnomah Publishers, 1995, 1999), p. 189.

[24] Matthew 11:28-29: "Come to Me, all who are weary and heavy-laden, and I will give you rest. Take My yoke upon you, and learn from Me, for I am gentle and humble in heart; and you shall find rest for your souls."

[25] Read my story and 31 others in **Exchanged Lives**, pp. 42-45.

fruit of the Spirit, godly love and Christ's character on earth). But I do it with trembling, fearing that someone will take these as chinning bars, struggling to measure up. Christ has already measured up, and He now wants, through our yielded and trusting spirit, soul and body, to reflect His life to others. It is His work.[26] We are the address but not the originators of the work. I used to pray that I'd be made stronger in order to obey the Lord. I now tell God that I'm incapable in myself to do His will. Instead of making me strong, I now ask Him to be my strength in union with Him, for Him to obey Scripture *through* me.

How can I focus on being more Christ-like?

The fact that I am not phrasing the question this way may puzzle you because you may have thought that Christ-likeness was the goal of all sincere Christians. And this is so close that it may seem like only a subtle distinction (yet in a way, it is so far from the real focus).

When we look closely at the question and notice the word "focus," we will have the key to a clear understanding of the inherent problem with this question. In reality our sole *focus* should be on *Christ* Himself, especially Him crucified and risen.[27] The

---

26 1 Thessalonians 5:18-19.

27 1 Corinthians 2:2; Hebrews 12:2. See also John Best, ***The Cross of Christ: The Center of Scripture, Your Life and Ministry*** (Garland, TX: Abundant Living Resources, 2007), pp. 28-30. www.abundantlivingresources.org

Christian life is the Christ-centered life, not merely a Christ-like-centered life. Charles McCall incisively observes:

> Some of the most Christ-like people I've known seldom, if ever, spoke about Christ-likeness. They spoke about Christ. Their focus was on Him and on living in an abiding relationship with Him wherein He was the main thing. Not Christ-likeness, but Christ; not the effect, but the cause was the orientation of their lives.[28]

Notice carefully above the place of the *cause* and the *effect*. Jesus Christ is the only One Who can produce Christ-likeness. Thus, He is the one on whom we need to focus, for us personally and in our ministry. Again McCall clarifies:

> We must take care that the creeds, convictions, and crusades of our life are not the main thing, the thing that drives us. Our life and ministry must truly be Christ, with every thing taught serving Him and pointing to Him... .

---

[28] Charles McCall, "Acting on the Truth: Christ vs. Christ-likeness" (Comfort, TX: Prayer letter from *His Hill*, 2004) p. 2.

> Why are we to preach Christ and not Christ-likeness? Because Christ is the cause of Christ-likeness![29]

So please, please remember in reading the rest of this paper that the great object of our lives is Jesus Christ Himself being given the trust and freedom to be Himself in us.

This is really the only key to keep living by faith when life gets really hard. Here is the prevailing perspective we need, from a student of Charles McCall: "I can persevere because it is Christ working in me, not me working in me. That's it! The issue is not what I am to do, but who He is prepared to be in me. That's why Christ-like people don't spend a lot of time talking about Christ-likeness. They talk about Christ."[30]

---

29 *Ibid.*
30 *Ibid.*

WHEN IS CHRIST BEING DISPLAYED IN US?

Now that we have seen the importance of the overall question and we have seen the four things it is not asking, let us develop the answer in more detail than earlier. I'm sure that as I do this some will think, as Chesterton did of his own writings, that these are "Elephantine adventures in the pursuit of the obvious."[31] However, these truths are obviously not very obvious to most of us because if they were, we would have more trust and peace due to this solution.

I will commence below to show the relationship between the fruit of the Spirit, godly love and the character of Christ in His earth walk. But I do so cautiously, concerned lest any of you will make any of these your goals, thinking they are the causes. *In reality Christ Himself* is the single goal; everything else is an effect, a side benefit.

---

31 G. K. Chesterton, **Orthodoxy** (New York: Doubleday, 1908, 1959), p. 4.

> **Christ is being seen in my life when His character is being displayed in me.**

His character can be simply seen in a comparison between His earthly life and death, the fruit of the Spirit and the qualities of godly (*agapē*) love.[32] The key to this interrelationship is that Jesus promised the disciples in the Upper Room[33] that His representative, the Holy Spirit, would reveal Christ to them (John 14:26) and glorify Christ in them (John 16:14). This Holy Spirit is also called "The Spirit of Christ."[34]

Therefore the fruit of that Spirit would indeed reveal and glorify Jesus Himself. This fruit, then, in the believer who knows Christ as his life[35] would be the answer to the question posed: When is Christ being displayed in us? I want this to be an encouragement

---

[32] I am not propounding that the whole of Christ's character qualities are found in this comparison. Jesus was the infinite God with all the attributes of the Godhead. At the same time He was a fully human man. No man's character can be encompassed in less than a dozen character qualities. So, what I am asserting is not a comprehensive catalogue of Christ's character but those qualities that He wants to reproduce and display in us.

[33] The Upper Room Discourse has been eloquently called "The Seedbed of Pauline Theology" by Lewis Sperry Chafer.

[34] The Holy Spirit, as well as being called "the **Spirit of Christ**" in Romans 8:9, is called "the **Spirit of Jesus**" in Acts 16:7 and "the **Spirit of Jesus Christ**" in Philippians 1:19

[35] "The **Spirit of life in Christ Jesus** has set me free from the law of sin and death" (Romans 8:2).

to those who are unnecessarily troubled about this. I am not concerned here with the person who may be trying to generate fruit on his own, rather than from Christ. Of course, false fruit may be generated by the flesh, but is it consistent? Does it have godly love at its core? Is it in accord with the further sequence of thought below?

Preview of the Principle

Let's take a simple example of this principle that Christ embodies the very qualities that God desires to produce in us through the indwelling Spirit of Christ.[36]

Since it is the Holy Spirit who pours out the love of God in our hearts,[37] we would expect that our indwelling God, Who is Love,[38] would be showing the aspects of love He told us about in 1 Corinthians 13:4-8. In fact, this grand chapter can be seen as a description of God Himself, as Bob George has said. He has a wonderful explanation of this in his first book, **Classic Christianity** (see page 198). He encourages us to substitute the word "God" for the word "love" every time we find it in 1 Corinthians 13.

This truth alone can transform your view of God and draw you closer to His caring heart.

---

36 Romans 8:9.
37 Romans 5:5.
38 1 John 4:8.

Let me further illustrate this principle. Christ is being seen when His character is displayed in me. I will show in the chart below the interconnection of the three things that show Christ's character:

The Fruit of the Spirit

> But the fruit of the Spirit is love, joy, peace, patience, kindness, goodness, faithfulness, gentleness, self-control; against such things there is no law. Galatians 5:22-23

It is noteworthy that some commentators, like Bob George saw in 1 Corinthians 13, see the fruit (note that it is singular) here as alluding or pointing to Christ Himself. For instance, Everett Harrison asserts:

> It is possible, also, that the singular [of "fruit"] may be intended to point to the person of Christ, in whom all these things are seen in their perfection. The Spirit seeks to produce these by reproducing Christ in the believer (cf. 4:19). Passages like Romans 13:14 suggest that the moral problems of redeemed men and women can be solved by the adequacy of Christ when He is appropriated by faith.[39]

---

39 Everett F. Harrison, ***The Wycliffe Bible Commentary*** (Chicago: Moody Press, 1962), p. 1296. Harrison does also say

So as Christ lives His life in us that life will be expressed in this same fruit seen in us, produced by Him (John 15:1-5). Donald K. Campbell, former president of Dallas Theological Seminary, also sees the life of Christ in the fruit, "In an ultimate sense this 'fruit' is simply the life of Christ lived out in a Christian. It also points to the method whereby Christ is formed in a believer (cf. 2 Corinthians 3:18; Philippians 1:21)."[40]

Therefore, I am including in the following chart this fruit that is "the normal outcropping of the Holy Spirit in us. It is a beautiful tree of fruit that Paul pictures here with nine luscious fruits on it."[41]

The Qualities of Godly Love (Agapē)

> Love is patient, love is kind, and is not jealous; love does not brag and is not arrogant, does not act unbecomingly; it does not seek its own, is not provoked, does not take into account a wrong suffered, does not rejoice in unrighteousness, but rejoices with the truth;

---

that the singular "tends to emphasize the unity and coherence of the Life in the Spirit as opposed to the disorganization and instability of life under the dictates of the flesh."

[40] Donald K. Campbell, ***The Bible Knowledge Commentary, New Testament Edition*** (Wheaton, IL: Victor Books, 1983), p. 608.

[41] Archibald T. Robertson, ***Word Pictures in the New Testament, The Epistles of Paul*** (Nashville: Broadman Press, 1931), vol. 4, p. 313.

> bears all things, believes all things, hopes all things, endures all things. Love never fails; but if there are gifts of prophecy, they will be done away; if there are tongues, they will cease; if there is knowledge, it will be done away. 1 Corinthians 13:4-8

The Greek word used here for love (as well as Galatians 5:22 and many other places in the New Testament) is *agapē*. Lenski portrays its meaning:

> [*Agapē*] is the love of intelligent comprehension united with corresponding blessed purpose. So God loved the world, understood all its depravity and purposed to remove it. He could not embrace the foul, stinking world in *philia,* but He did love it with *agapē* and sent his Son to cleanse it. Jesus did not love the Pharisees with *philia* and does not ask us so to love our enemies. It is *agapē* that He asks, the love that understands the hatefulness of the enemy and purposes to remove it.[42]

Leon Morris says that 1 Corinthians 13 is "of singular beauty and power ... the greatest, strongest, deepest

---

42 R. C. H. Lenski, ***The Interpretation of St. Paul's Epistles to the Galatians, to the Ephesians, and to the Philippians*** (Minneapolis: Augsburg Publishing House, 1937), p. 291. Lenski has many other sagacious observations on the Greek text.

thing Paul ever wrote."[43] As I have already pointed out, some commentators agree with me in seeing Christ Himself in this description of love. "When we think of the qualities of this love as Paul portrays them, we can see them realized in the life of Jesus Himself."[44]

Therefore, Paul's description of *agapē* love is included in the chart on the next page as one of the wonderful ways Christ's character can be seen in us.

The Life and Death of Christ on Earth as They Illustrate Fruit and Love

As we look at Jesus' life and death we do indeed see the fruit of the Spirit and the facets of godly love.[45] I have put these on the chart below as they occurred to me. You probably can think of others. I hope that those I have included will demonstrate to you the correlation between His life and the summaries of His character in Galatians 5:22-23 and 1 Corinthians 13:4-8.

---

[43] Leon Morris, ***The First Epistle of Paul to the Corinthians*** (Grand Rapids: Wm. B. Eerdmans Publishing Company, 1958), p. 180.

[44] William Barclay, ***The Letters to the Corinthians*** (Philadelphia:The Westminster Press, 1975), p. 125.

[45] Again I would seek to clarify that these lists do not encompass all of Jesus' character or actions. There are aspects of Jesus that will not usually be seen in us. For instance, we are not all powerful, all knowing, equal with God the Father and Holy Spirit, never sinning, dying a vicarious, substitutional death for others.

I trust that you will recognize and then remember He possessed one goal: to go to the cross. He repeated over and over "My hour has not come!" In the shadow of Calvary He declared, "Father, My hour has come" (John 17:1). His goal was not to display the fruit of the Spirit and godly love. He couldn't help but to do these because He was dependent always on His Father.

Thus do not read any further until you go back to the front to reread and understand the Prologue!

THE CHARACTER OF CHRIST: FIRST CHART

Fruit of the Spirit	Qualities of Godly love (*Agapē*)	The Life of Christ on Earth
Galatians 5:22-23	1 Corinthians 13:4-8	Examples from The Gospels and Epistles
The Holy Spirit is the Spirit of Christ who reveals and glorifies Him. The results are His fruit. Gal. 5:22-23 has been called "The Shortest Life of Christ."	Since God is Love (1 John 4:8b) and since Christ is God (John 1:1c), the love described here shows that Christ is producing it in the trusting believer. It can be paralleled to the fruit of the Spirit since that also is generated by Christ within.	These beautiful characteristics of the Lord Jesus are seen in the life He lived here on earth. The life of Christ within the believer will also display these same attributes, an awesome thought to consider, believe and live.

| The fruit of the Spirit is LOVE | Love does not brag, is not arrogant. | <ul><li>Jesus loved His own to the uttermost, (John 13:1) stooping to wash their feet as a servant (13:5; cf. to Mark 10:45: "the Son of Man did not come to be served but to serve …").</li><li>Jesus loved and laid down His life for His friends (John 15:13) and for His enemies (Romans 5:6-10, cf. to Mark 10:45-6: "… and to give His life a ransom for many").</li><li>Jesus loved all, great and small, upright and sinful.</li><li>Jesus loves us enough to take us also to the cross with Him, crucifying the old man and raising us with Him making us acceptable and accepted (Romans 6:4-6, 15:7).</li><li>Jesus was meek and lowly (Matthew 11:29, 21:5) and though He was the eternal Son of God and Creator of the universe, He never bragged about Himself attributing all about Himself to the Father (John 5:19-24,36; 6:37-39; 7:16-18, 28; 8:28, 38, 42; Philippians 2:5-8) and took the place of a humble servant.</li></ul> |

THE CHARACTER OF CHRIST: FIRST CHART

	Love does not brag, is not arrogant.	‣ He was never arrogant even when given the opportunity to claim that His kingdom was of this world, telling Jews to "render unto God what is God's and unto Caesar what is Caesar's (Mark 12:17; Luke 20:25).
	Love does not take into account a wrong suffered	‣ Jesus responded at times to false accusations with factual, not vindictive answers (Matthew 22:23-40; 26:62-68; Luke 20:19-44). ‣ He welcomed both Zaccheus and Matthew, though they were despised tax collectors who had done their fellow Israelites much harm (Luke 19:4-10; Matthew 9:9-13). ‣ Christ, when being unjustly arrested healed the ear of the high priest's servant which Peter had cut off defending Jesus against the "wrong suffered" (Luke 22:50-1). ‣ Jesus prayed for those crucifying Him, "Father, forgive them, for they do not know what they are doing" (Luke 23:34).

The fruit of the Spirit is JOY	Love does not rejoice in unrighteousness but rejoices in the truth.	‣ Christ, instead of rejoicing about their unrighteousness, rebuked the Pharisees in Matthew 23 and many other places. ‣ He made righteous the humble penitent who prayed "God be merciful to me, a sinner" rather than the self-righteous Pharisee (Luke 18:31). ‣ He hated the unrighteousness of making His Father's house a den of thieves and twice cleansed the Temple of the money changers and sellers (Mark 11:15; John 2:15). ‣ "Jesus rejoiced greatly in the Holy Spirit" (Luke 10:21). ‣ He willingly endured the cross, thinking little of the shame, because of the joy set before Him (Hebrews 12:2) of seeing many of us becoming righteous in Him and becoming His brethren (2 Corinthians 5:21; Hebrews 2:12; Romans 8:29).
The fruit of the Spirit is PEACE	Love is not provoked	‣ Jesus responded to the repeated needling of the Jewish leaders with facts, not invectives (e.g. Matthew 22:23-40; Luke 20:19-44).

The fruit of the Spirit is PEACE	**Love is not provoked**	• When He was accused and taunted at His trials He did not become provoked. He answered simply and gently or not at all (Matthew 26:62-8; Luke 22:66-70). • When Christ was beaten, ridiculed and crucified, He was not provoked but laid down His life for us willingly (Isaiah 53:4-7; John 10:11, 17-18).
The fruit of the Spirit is PATIENCE	**Love is patient**	• Christ waited about 30 years before He entered His public ministry. During His public ministry He did not do some things that would have promoted Him to more preeminence because, as He said, "My hour is not come" (John 2:4, 7:6). • Jesus put up with the fearful, self-seeking and strife ridden disciples, only chiding them for having "little faith." He deeply loved them and patiently taught them in spite of their faults, knowing that the cross, resurrection and Pentecost would later empower them to follow His teaching.

The fruit of the Spirit is PATIENCE	Love is patient	‣ As pointed out before (under "is not provoked"), Jesus' response to the needling, accusations and taunting of some of the Jewish leaders and others was a patient response: factual, gentle, simple and sometimes silent.
The fruit of the Spirit is KINDNESS	Love is kind	‣ Jesus was known as a kind man as He healed the sick, restored sight to the blind, ministered to the poor and brokenhearted and raised the dead. He proclaimed at the beginning of His public ministry, *"The Spirit of the Lord is upon Me, Because He anointed Me to preach the gospel to the poor. He has sent Me to proclaim release to the captives, And recovery of sight to the blind, To set free those who are downtrodden, To proclaim the favorable year of the Lord"* (Luke 4:18-19). ‣ He was not too busy for the children or too aloof for the lepers.

| The fruit of the Spirit is **GOODNESS** | **Love does not seek its own** | ‣ The paramount way that Jesus did "not seek [His] own" and was good was in not seeking to save His own life but to lay it down for even His enemies, we who were dead in our sins, self-centered, godless and unable to save ourselves (Ephesians 2:1-9; Romans 5:5-9).
‣ His unselfish goodness did not stop there; He crucified us with Him so He could raise us with Him, indwelt by Him and thus "saved by His life" (Romans 5:10; Ephesians 2:4-8).
‣ This presenting of Himself as a servant at the cross was foreshadowed as He washed the disciples' feet and gave them loving, parting comfort and instructions, which they would only understand later (John 13-16).
‣ His goodness was seen in all He did and said and continues to this day for His own (John 17; Hebrews 4:15-16). |

The fruit of the Spirit is FAITHFULNESS	**Love endures all things, never fails**	▸ Christ always did His Father's will (John 4:34), being obedient unto death, enduring even death of the cross (Philippians 2:8). No amount of suffering would cause His love to fail, even to the point of becoming a sin offering for every sin of us all, to make us the righteousness of God in Him (2 Corinthians 5:21; Hebrews 12:2).
	Love believes all things	▸ Jesus never flinched in His belief that His mission was to save us through the full work of the cross. He ever entrusted Himself to His Father. Entrustment meant He believed His Father knew best (1 Peter 2:23-24). ▸ He entrusted His followers with the Great Commission (Matthew 28:18-20). He so believed in the empowering of the Holy Spirit (Acts 1:8), Who would reveal Christ to them (John 16:14), that He gave this small group marching orders that extended to the whole world (Mark 16:15).

	Love hopes all things	• Though tempted three times in the wilderness, He maintained His hope in the Father for all He needed (Matthew 4, Luke 4). • He so knew the power of God that He told people to sin no more, to faint not and to remain faithful in their own persecutions and temptations. • He presented Himself as the reason for the disciples' hope for a future place with Him forever (John 14–16).
The fruit of the Spirit is GENTLE-NESS	**Love bears all things**	• Jesus was gentle with the outcasts of society: harlots, the woman taken in adultery, the lepers, and the tax collectors. • His patience in bearing all things extended to His close followers who had irritatingly little faith and were often jockeying for more prominence. (Matthew 8:26; 20:20-28; Luke 22:24; John 13:2-17). • Jesus responded to false accusations, not vindictively, but with gentle facts and questions. Truly He was one who bore "all things" including the cross.

The fruit of the Spirit is GENTLE-NESS	**Love bears all things**	‣ See also the earlier section on "peace" and "patience."
The fruit of the Spirit is SELF CONTROL	**Love does not act unbecomingly**	‣ Christ brought all that was human within Him under the control of all that was divine. He never unbecomingly acted inappropriately. He gave all credit and glory to His empowering, commanding Father "I do nothing on My own initiative," He declared in John 5:30. ‣ When faced with "drinking the cup" of God's wrath against the sin of the whole world and thus being separated from Him, Jesus put Himself under the Father's control: "Not My will but Your will be done" (Matthew 26:39-42). ‣ Jesus was respectful of the High Priest at His trial and never lashed back at those who were lashing Him.

The above material should be more than an interesting chart comparing Jesus life to Galatians 5:22-23 and 1 Corinthians 13:4-8. It has meant much more than that to me! It has shown me that sometimes I am too unheeding of my constant need of Jesus, too smug and self-reliant.

It has shown me that, in such a state, I am not displaying Christ, the One Who is alone worthy of full attention. He is the One Who reflects God's glory from and to the Father.

I have also been reminded (and I need reminding often) that only Christ's life, given full reign in me, can produce the fruit of the Spirit and *agapē* love. It is futile to try to produce these independently, even if I am well-intended in my attempts. I am sadly inadequate and sorely misguided in these self-generated pursuits of virtue.

But I am also greatly encouraged by the information on the chart from the Word of God: by trusting Christ, His life, His love, and His fruit will supernaturally be expressed in and through me.[46] There will be more on this near the end of this paper.

A Surprising Discovery

While writing the preceding material, which I had developed weeks before, this thought occurred to me: "There is another list of virtues in the New Testament, the 'Beatitudes' in the Sermon on the

---
46 2 Corinthians 2:14; Romans 15:17.

Mount. Could it be that there are parallels between these and the other lists of virtues?" At first I dismissed this as just being a far-fetched idea or one that would take quite a stretch to make them fit with the others.

However, I have learned not to dismiss so quickly the thoughts that come to me spontaneously.[47] Sometimes I've found that they are the promptings of the Holy Spirit with my spirit.[48] So they deserve to be checked out.[49] As I studied these Beatitudes, comparing them to the features found in the chart above, I was amazed at the correlation.

Concerning the Sermon on the Mount itself, there is great difference of opinion as to where it fits (or does not fit) for the Christian living under grace.[50]

---

47 Mark and Ruth Virkler, **Dialogue With God** (Gainsville, FL: Bridge Logos Publishers, 1986), pp. 27-32.

48 See John Best, **Exploring the Treasure of Your New Human Spirit** (Garland, TX: Abundant Living Resources 2011), note the section on "The Daily Life of Your Human Spirit." www.AbundantLivingResources.org.

49 Virkler, pp. 132-140 and Best, **Your New Spirit**, under section above, "Advice and Caution about Living by Your Spirit."

50 Concerning the application of the Sermon on the Mount, there is great difference of opinion as to where it fits (or does not fit) for the Christian living under grace. These opinions range widely.

   a. **Here and now commands of a deep spiritual morality.**
      For instance John Broadus claims:
      "In this discourse He sets forth the characteristics of those who are to be subjects of this reign and share

Whichever of these opinions about the Sermon one adopts, it seems reasonable that the great principles in much of it are transhistorical and transdispensational and thus of value to all godly people.

But still there is the nagging, frustrating awareness that, at my best, I can never live up to any of the

---

the privileges connected with it, and urges upon them various duties. In particular, He clearly exhibits the relation of His teachings to the moral law, in order to correct any notion that He proposed to set the law aside, or to relax its rigor, when, on the contrary He came He came to inculcate not merely an external but a deeply spiritual morality." John A. Broadus, ***An American Commentary on the New Testament Volume 1, Matthew*** (Philadelphia: The American Baptist Publication Society, 1886), pp. 84, 85.

Donald Campbell seems to agree partially: "While the passage must be understood in the light of the offer of the Messianic kingdom, the sermon applies to Jesus' followers today for it demonstrates the standard of righteousness God demands of His people." Ed. by John F. Walvoord and Roy B. Zuck, ***The Bible Knowledge Commentary*** (Wheaton, IL: SP Publications, 1983), p. 28.

b. Primarily the future reign of Christ on earth.

Charles Ryrie notes that a reference to the present day is not, in his opinion, the primary emphasis of the sermon:

Now, what does dispensationalism say about the Sermon? It says two things: (1) The Sermon is **primarily** related to the Messianic kingdom. [By "Messianic Kingdom" Dr. Ryrie refers to the 1000 year (millennial) reign of Christ in the future (Revelation 20:5 and many Old Testament prophecies).] (2) Like all Scripture, the Sermon is applicable to believers in this age...[But] the literal obedience to the laws is impossible today. Charles C. Ryrie, **Dispensationalism Today** (Chicago: Moody Press, 1965), p. 107.

principles in this sermon.[51] It is good for me to see this![52] When I do, I know that only Christ can live up to His own teachings!

c. A demonstration of the futility of human works to gain righteousness with God.

Tom Weaver sees a greater purpose in the sermon than even telling us about conduct in the future kingdom or today:

They call this the Sermon on the Mount because Jesus delivered it from a hillside, but I would suggest it should be called the Sermon on the Fault, because the Lord's purpose was to demonstrate the utter futility of ever measuring up to God's demands. Jesus graphically demonstrates over and over again how many faults we really have, and how far short we fall of God's perfect standard. Tom Weaver, John Souter, **The Gospel Solution** (Bremerton, WA: Thomas Weaver and John Souter, 1999), p. 137.

Weaver and Souter cite many of Jesus' teachings and parables as having this same purpose. They do this without being pedantic or presumptuous.

For a similar view (that the sermon was designed to show all the futility of a works-based justification or sanctification) see Gillham **What God Wishes**, pp. 127-135, 143-155. "By teaching law, Jesus dropped His listeners into a deep cistern with slick walls... Jesus' *agapē* goal was to produce a hunger for eternal life..." p. 145.

51 For a non-Christian, Christ's teachings are not just frustrating; they are deadly, if he does not submit himself to the work of the cross of Christ. In his book, **The Cross**, Martyn Lloyd-Jones relates that many people today would insist that the cross is not really important. According to many, all we need to do is follow Christ's teaching and His example.

But as Lloyd-Jones says, without the cross, Jesus' teaching and His example only lead to condemnation. "If you only preach the teaching of the Lord Jesus Christ, not only do you not solve the problem of mankind, in a sense you even aggravate it. You are preaching nothing but utter condemnation because nobody can ever carry it out." D. Martyn Lloyd-Jones, **The Cross** (Westchester, IL: Crossway Books, 1986), p. 20.

52 Remember that it was also good for me to see that I could not emulate the character of Christ, generate the fruit of the Spirit or produce *agapē* love myself! Then I see my need of Christ.

Now, taking all of this together, what should result from Jesus and His character being lived out through us? It is that we become in our attitudes and actions those who are being blessed by being gentle, merciful, pure in heart, peacemakers and so on. So Jesus produces in us the very character He said would bring us blessedness![53] And we are blessed as He, through us, blesses others.

Here are the parallels that I've seen. I admit that the fit is not perfect. For instance, I've not been able to find where the "poor in spirit" and "those who mourn" fit (Matthew 5:3-4). Perhaps a more clever or imaginative mind than mine can find the correlation. If so, I'd love to hear from you.

I present below the previous chart, reducing the details on the life and death of Christ for the sake of brevity only. I have added a final column to it with the Beatitudes that seem to relate to the way Christ is recognized. Note that Jesus in grace makes us into the kind of people who are blessed in a way that the world cannot understand. For instance, it makes no sense to those with a dead spirit to God and no eternal perspective to see blessings in being insulted, persecuted and having all kinds of evil things said against you falsely for Christ's sake (Matthew 5:11). The man of this world sees only blessings in political and religious freedom, a good family and prosperity.

---

[53] But do bear in mind that our blessedness is not limited to these for we have been "blessed with all spiritual blessings in the heavenlies in Christ Jesus" (Ephesians 1:3).

THE CHARACTER OF CHRIST: SECOND CHART

Fruit of the Spirit	Qualities of Godly Love (*Agapē*)	Life of Christ on Earth	The Beatitudes
Galatians 5:22-23	1 Corinthians 13:4-8	The Gospels and Epistles	Matthew 5:3-12
The Holy Spirit is the Spirit of Christ who reveals and glorifies Him. The results are His fruit. Galatians 5:22-23 has been called "The Shortest Life of Christ."	Since God is love (1 John 4:8b) and since Christ is God (John 1:1c), the love here described shows that Christ is producing it in the trusting believer. It can be paralleled to the fruit of the Spirit since that also is generated by Christ within.	The life of Christ within the believer will be reflecting the things seen to the left. Here these same beautiful characteristics of the Lord Jesus are seen in the life He lived here on earth.	Christ produces these results in believers that bring them blessedness.

The fruit of the Spirit is LOVE	Love does not brag, is not arrogant.	Jesus loved and laid down His life for His friends (John 15:13) and for His enemies (Romans 5:6-10).	Although no specific Beatitude has the word "love" they all reflect a humble, others oriented attitude of godly love!
	Love does not take into account a wrong suffered	Christ prayed for those crucifying Him.	"Blessed are those who are persecuted for the sake of righteousness" (v. 10a).
The fruit of the Spirit is JOY	Does not rejoice in unrighteousness but rejoices in the truth.	"Jesus rejoiced greatly in the Holy Spirit" (Luke 10:21). He willingly endured the cross, thinking little of the shame, because of the joy set before Him (Hebrews 12:2).	"Rejoice, and be glad, for your reward in heaven is great; for so they persecuted the prophets who were before you" (v. 12).

The fruit of the Spirit is PEACE	**Love is not provoked**	When Christ was beaten, ridiculed and crucified, He was not provoked but laid down His life for us willingly (Isaiah 53:4-7; John 10:17-18).	"Blessed are the peacemakers, for they shall be called the sons of God" (v.9). Note the idea expressed here: "They shall be called."
The fruit of the Spirit is PATIENCE	**Love is patient**	Jesus' response to the needling, accusations and taunting of some of the Jewish leaders and others was a patient response; factual, gentle, simple and sometimes silent.	Blessed are those who are persecuted for the sake of righteousness, for theirs is the kingdom of heaven" (v. 10).

The fruit of the Spirit is KINDNESS	Love is kind	"The Spirit of the Lord is upon Me, Because He anointed Me to preach the gospel to the poor. He has sent Me to proclaim release to the captives, And recovery of sight to the blind, To set free those who are downtrodden, To proclaim the favorable year of the Lord" (Luke 4:18-19).	"Blessed are the merciful, for they shall receive mercy" (v. 7).
The fruit of the Spirit is GOODNESS	Love does not seek its own	Jesus crucified us with Him so He could raise us with Him, indwelt by Him and thus "saved by His life" (Romans 5:10; Ephesians 2:4-8) and made righteous (2 Corinthians 5:21).	"Blessed are those who hunger and thirst for righteousness, for they shall be satisfied" (v. 6).

THE CHARACTER OF CHRIST: SECOND CHART

The fruit of the Spirit is FAITH-FUL-NESS	Love endures all things, never fails		"Blessed are those who are persecuted for the sake of righteousness, for theirs is the kingdom of heaven. Blessed are you when men cast insults at you, and persecute you and say all kinds of evil against you falsely on account of Me. Rejoice and be glad, for your reward in heaven is great, for so they persecuted the prophets who were before you" (vv. 10-12).
	Love believes all things	Christ ever entrusted Himself to His Father.	"Blessed are the pure in heart, for they shall see God" (v. 8).
	Love hopes all things	He hoped in His Father. He is our hope.	

The fruit of the Spirit is GENTLENESS	Love bears all things	Jesus was gentle with the outcasts of society. His patience in bearing all things extended to His close followers who had irritatingly little faith and were often jockeying for more prominence. He bore all things in His trial and crucifixion.	"Blessed are the gentle, for they shall inherit the earth" (v. 5).
The fruit of the Spirit is SELF CONTROL	Love does not act unbecomingly	Christ brought all that was human within Him under the control of all that was divine.	All of the above actions and attitudes imply self-control.

The above chart shows that as Jesus and His character is being lived out in and through us, something happens that we could *never* produce ourselves. We become, in our attitudes and actions, those who are blessed. Jesus Christ within us generates the very qualities that He promised would bring us blessedness.

This is the grace of living in the New Covenant: *God wills within us*[54] *what pleases Him. He then directs*[55] *and empowers*[56] *us to do the very things that delight Him.*[57] *As we do, He rewards us*[58] *for His very own work.*[59] Is it any wonder that Jesus Christ is called "the Author and Finisher of our faith" (Hebrews 12:2)?

A Living Lesson

Dan Stone explains very clearly the link between how Christ looked and how we can learn to reflect Him:

> What does the life of God living through us look like? For our primary example we have to go no further than the Gospels. Jesus said, "Come to Me, all who are weary and heavy-laden, and I will give you rest. Take my yoke upon you and learn from Me… and you will find rest for your souls. For My yoke is easy and My burden is light" (Matthew 11:28-30).

---

54 Philippians 2:13.
55 Ezekiel 36:27.
56 2 Corinthians 3:6.
57 Philippians 3:13b.
58 Hebrews 11:6; Matthew 5:12; 1 Corinthians 3:14.
59 Philippians 3:13a.

I often wondered, "What did He mean, 'Learn from Me?'" As I looked through the Gospel of John, I found the answer. I saw Jesus making statements over and over like:

"I don't do anything of Myself."

"I only do what I see the Father do."

"I only speak what I hear from the Father."

"The works that I do, they're not My works; they're the Father's works Who dwells in Me."

When Jesus said, "Learn from Me," He meant to learn from Him how He lived. And how did He live? He lived out of the Father. He didn't have any other secret.[60]

Living Pictures

Perhaps when we wonder the most about Jesus being seen in us, we have the greatest opportunity: to have Him so inhabit us that we forget about our self-absorption and self-analysis and just live life where He has put us. Then we can let God take care of Christ shining through us. That is the living picture He desires for our lives.

---

60 Dan Stone and Greg Smith, ***The Rest of the Gospel*** (Richardson, TX: One Press, 2000), p. 60.

As He does we will bring God glory as well as attract others to Christ. A vivid illustration of this is found in this story by Tony Campolo:

Joe's Story

Joe was a drunk who was miraculously converted at a Bowery mission. Prior to his conversion, he had gained the reputation of being a dirty wino for whom there was no hope, only a miserable existence in the ghetto. But following his conversion to a new life with God, everything changed. Joe became the most caring person that anyone associated with the mission had ever known. Joe spent his days and nights hanging out at the mission, doing whatever needed to be done. There was never anything that he was asked to do that he considered beneath him. Whether it was cleaning up the vomit left by some violently sick alcoholic or scrubbing toilets after careless men left the men's room filthy, Joe did what was asked with a smile on his face and a seeming gratitude for the chance to help. He could be counted on to feed feeble men who wandered off the street and into the mission, and to undress and tuck into bed men who were too out of it to take care of themselves.

One evening, when the director of the mission was delivering his evening evangelistic message to the usual crowd of still and sullen men with drooped heads, there was one man who looked up, came down the aisle to the alter, and knelt to pray, crying out for God to help him to change. The repentant drunk kept shouting, "Oh God! Make me like Joe! Make me like Joe! Make me like Joe! Make me like Joe!"

The director of the mission leaned over and said to the man, "Son, I think it would be better if you prayed, 'Make me like *Jesus*.'"

The man looked up at the director with a quizzical expression on his face and asked, "Is He like Joe?"[61]

Christ being seen in someone's life is so compelling!

Although I see great hope in Christ's power and inward presence to make me one who lets Him shine through me, I do not think I let Him do this as consistently as I could. So I see myself as one who is in process.

---

61 Alice Gray, ***Stories from the Heart,*** p. 28.

My Friend Ray

The Lord has been very good to me in bringing several people into my life who are further along in this process than I am.[62] I am concluding this study with one of them. As I have observed this man over several years, he strikes me as one in whom Christ lives with such freedom that he actually reminds me of Jesus.

Others have concluded this as well. One of our Exchanged Life Ministries Texas staff who spent three weeks with him, day and night, in our Advanced Training and Teaching in Pagosa Springs, Colorado, told him in our closing session, "Ray, as I think of what Jesus might be like if He were physically present with us, I think He would be very much like you: loving and caring in what He said and did."

Now I want you to know something more about Ray's present and past. In the present he is not a mealy-mouthed, Casper Milk Toast, wimpy type of man. Though kind, he is straight forward and not passive. But in the past Ray was not always a walking personification of Christ.[63] He told me that when he

---

[62] See especially these stories in **Exchanged Lives**: Lee LeFebre (pp. 28-30), Richard Flaten (pp. 38-40), Jamie Lash (pp. 48-50), and Ray Rodgers (pp. 51-53). Ray's story is condensed later in this paper.

[63] Note in Ray's story following this principle: *While the self-resourced life (the flesh) is working for us, we will not seek*

was in college he was self-centered, critical inwardly and outwardly, and his tongue was acrimonious and sarcastic.[64]

What transformed Ray from this to one who is Jesus to people? I'll let Ray tell his own story:

> After struggling in the real estate market, the Lord showed me that my identity was rooted in my success in business. When the business declined, my weakness surfaced. I arrived home one evening in despair. I threw myself on the floor before my wife and stated, "If this is all there is to the Christian life then I have had enough."
>
> At the suggestion of my sweet bride I called my Sunday school teacher. He asked me a basic question, "What does the cross of Christ mean to you?" After a short pause, I wondered what relevance that had to my current situation. I responded with an explanation of salvation that would have made my other teachers proud. After another pause my mentor asked,

---

anything better.

64 For another account of one who was also like this and was transformed by learning what it was to be "in Christ" and to have Christ living in him see Bill Gillham, ***Lifetime Guarantee***, pp. 53-66, 119-20, 155-161. I would certainly include this brother in Christ with those in the preceding footnote as one who is further along in this process than I am.

"What else does the cross mean?" I knew I was about to receive a nugget of truth at this point. My friend began to share the "full" result of salvation that included not only the blood of Christ that granted forgiveness, but also my co-crucifixion and co-resurrection with Christ. These were truths I had never seen before. I began to study Romans, chapters 6, 7, 8 and Galatians, chapter 2. As I studied these passages I saw the "Hope of Glory" and His touch on my life.

As I was involved with a Sunday school class and teacher that continually taught of the exchanged life truths, I witnessed first hand the transforming power of the cross in my life and the lives of other folks who have been touched by Jesus.

Although I had been aware of Exchanged Life Ministries Texas when John Best was led to begin the ministry in 1985, it was not until the spring of '92 that my wife and I attended our first Exchanged Life Conference. The Lord used it mightily to clarify further questions we had, as well as to reveal a more intense desire to let Christ reign in more areas of our lives. Having an intense dose of these truths proved to be a tremendous help to me and my wife.

I then proceeded to attend the Exchanged Life Workshop where I gained the insight in how to lead hurting folks back to the cross in a concise and effective way. Since then, the Lord has given me many opportunities to disciple people and to teach Sunday School classes where the practical application of these truths have been communicated and more believers have been set free. I recently benefited greatly from the Exchanged Life Advanced Training and Teaching. This took me much deeper in learning to abide in my life in God's sweet Son (John 15:1-5).

Today the Lord is continually revealing areas of bondage in my life while overwhelmingly allowing me the privilege of "experiencing" His love and care, not just "talking" about it. The harder the tests have become the more His life has been revealed.

I have come to see the importance of surrendering "my" rights and expectations in order to receive His and that is what pleases Him most. The world cannot relate to a "broken and contrite spirit," but it is precious to our loving Father.[65]

---

65 Adapted from Best, ***Exchanged Lives***, pp. 51-53.

As Ray did, you too can let the beautiful life and character of Christ be seen in you. As you depend upon Christ, He will minister to others through you.

Although I also have the following paragraph earlier, it is worth repeating it as the conclusion of the book.

Isn't it wonderful to be under grace?[66] In the New Covenant,[67] God wills within us[68] what pleases Him. He then directs[69] and empowers[70] us to do the very things that delight Him[71]. As we do and Christ is seen is us,[72] He rewards us for His very own work[73] through us.[74] The triune God is working in and through it all. To Him alone be the glory!

I like your Christ;

I do not like your Christians;

I wish they were more like Christ.

Gandhi

SCRIPTURES ABOUT LOVE

"... I show you a more excellent way.

Though I speak with the tongues of men and of angels, but have not love, I have become sounding brass or a clanging cymbal. And though I have the gift of prophecy, and understand all mysteries and all knowledge, and though I have all faith, so that I could remove mountains, but have not love, I am nothing. And though I bestow all my goods to feed the poor, and though I give my body to be burned, but have not love, it profits me nothing.

Love suffers long and is kind; love does not envy; love does not parade itself, is not puffed up; does not behave rudely, does not seek its own, is not provoked, thinks no evil; does not rejoice in iniquity, but rejoices in the truth; bears all things, believes all things, hopes all things, endures all things.

Love never fails. But whether there are prophecies, they will fail; whether there are tongues, they will cease; whether there is knowledge, it will vanish away. For we know in part and we prophesy in part. But when that which is perfect has come, then that which is in part will be done away.

When I was a child, I spoke as a child, I understood as a child, I thought as a child; but when I became a man, I put away childish things. For now we see in a mirror, dimly, but then face to face. Now I know in part, but then I shall know just as I also am known.

And now abide faith, hope, love, these three; but the greatest of these is love."

1 Corinthians 12:31-13:13

"A new commandment I give to you, that you love one another; as I have loved you, that you also love one another. By this all will know that you are My disciples, if you have love for one another."

John 13:34,35

TESTIMONIES

Testimony of Carolyn Best

I came to know Christ as my Savior at the age of seven. I was afraid I would be left behind if Christ returned or my folks died. Scared and knowing I needed something outside myself I one night came to my mother and she led me to know Jesus. In simple faith and trust, I entrusted my eternal destiny to Him.

I really loved the Lord so much that I wanted to please Him and I loved my parents so much that I wanted to please them as well. When I saw some of my older brothers and sisters hurt my mom and dad, I determined in my heart that I would be different. I would live right. And so I began my struggle to "live *for* Jesus."

Actually I lived a pretty good Christian life. I taught Sunday School, sang in the choir, went out on visitation, attended every church service, and even lead others to know Jesus. In fact, I did so well I thought within myself that I was really good. As a teenager I dedicated my life to full- time Christian work and began attending Bible college. At first I was very enthusiastic, but by the end of my last year I knew something within me was missing. And in the meantime I had fallen in love with John Best and married him. I went through a period my last year of Bible college of deep depression that continued off and on for several years.

The Pit of Depression

We moved to Dallas, Texas after college so John could attend Dallas Theological Seminary. Away from everything and everyone familiar, my depression deepened. By the end of John's second year of seminary, I was totally bedridden, depressed and in tremendous pain from a back injury. I was angry with God. Although I had dedicated my life to Him for full-time Christian work, I had served Him faithfully year after year, I had lived a good life, yet He was allowing me to be incapacitated and in unbelievable pain. Why? Why? Why? I began to doubt the very existence of God. How could there be a God of love? I had done my best and He was rewarding me with pain I could not bear.

Relief was all I wanted. So I began my drop into taking pill after pill just to relieve the pain. I lived for the hour when I could take another pill. Without me realizing it or even caring I became hooked on pain killers. In this semi-conscious state I lost my desire to live. I wanted out of this horrible joke my life had become. I could not face the solid wall of pain that engrossed me from head to toe. I knew that if something did not happen to help me I was finished. I could not go on like this indefinitely.

Lifted Out of the Pit

I began to honestly face myself with truth. If there really was a God, couldn't He help me? In brokenness I confessed my sin to God. I saw clearly my spiritual pride. Now I could do nothing for God. I had to take from Him. I needed Him. I could not live without something beyond myself to really change me. I humbled myself, admitted my sin and asked God to transform me.

Jesus met me right there in such a real way that I will never doubt the existence of God again. Right in the midst of my pain I had a peace and joy in my heart. I went from deep depression to peace and joy in a short time. Tears of relief and joy filled my eyes time after time. God had performed a miracle within my heart, but He did not immediately change my circumstances. My intense back pain continued for months.

Set Upon the Rock

Now that I have learned more about what actually happened that day when I personally encountered Christ, I have a clearer idea of just how He changed me. Nevertheless the fact that He had changed me was startling to both me and my husband.

John told me that some deep-seated attitudes that I had were changed 180 degrees: for instance, instead of resenting being in Dallas and away from my family, I now really wanted to be there. Instead of fearing being different than the people I worked with I now really desired not just to be different but to reach out to them with Christ's love.

Because I didn't understand exactly what had happened to me or how I could consistently walk in victory, I for many years had an up and down Christian life. I didn't realize that Christ could give me His victory in even the small things. I thought He only cared about the big things. Time after time when the pressures of raising children were added to another battle with pain, I would become angry, discouraged and disappointed in myself. I thought some things still depended on me rather than upon Jesus who indwelt me.

How did I finally get to the place where I understood enough of the truly biblical concept of Christian living so I could consistently appropriate it in my life?

My Way Established

Let me take you back to 1984. I was once again suffering severe pain, seeking for God to work in my heart to touch me once again with His power and strength. John brought home some books by Charles Solomon, *The Handbook to Happiness* and *The Ins and Out of Rejection*. I read completely through those books in just a day or two and I knew immediately that this explained what I had experienced several years ago before. Now I knew how to consistently live with Christ as my life and I knew how to share it with someone else. God has used me both with groups and individuals to help people and I've seen God work miracles in other lives. It's exciting to know I can't change anyone, I don't have the power to change people. But I know Christ has changed my life and I've seen Him change others.

My "Know It All" Attitude

My biggest problem was (and still is at times) my "know it all" attitude. I thought I knew what was best for myself, my family, my church, unsaved people and the whole world as far as that was concerned. But I failed time and time again when the pressure was too great. Jesus in His love was breaking me down. When I clearly saw that I could not make it in my own fleshly efforts, I humbled myself, admitted my sin, counted on my death with Christ to sin and allowed Christ to live His life through me (Romans 6:11).

The flesh is still with me and tries to regain control in my life but I have the power in Christ to not just overcome, but to live in real victory.

The flesh wants to tell people where to get off, how they should change things to make their life better. In contrast, Christ in me wants me to admit my anger, to be honest about the way I feel. In love

Christ in me wants to point the way to a better life which is never found in fleshly efforts to live right or to change habits, but is only found when Christ is allowed to rule and reign.

The flesh wants me to *always* be right and not listen to someone else. Christ wants me to be open to the fact I could be wrong in my personal judgement, that other people may be right, and since it is not a matter of moral right or wrong, why not try it someone else's way. Even if they fail, I will not criticize the person who is down.

The flesh wants me to imitate good works. But Christ wants me to let Him live His life through me and good works will be the natural result.

Freed from Fighting

The flesh tries to control others. As a child I was in many physical battles with my older brothers. Over the years I hardened myself to the point of becoming very controlling and mean to others around me. My sister, Linda, who is two years younger than I, recalls one Christmas when we both got identical dolls for Christmas. She says I smashed the head of her new doll and tore off the arms. I had turned from being the victim to being the victimizer at a certain time in my life. I became a fighter. I honestly could not recall these things very clearly until a recent session where I was helping someone else. God helped me to trace this flesh pattern all through my life up to today. I had to face the overwhelming truth of my guilt and shame. But along with this was an overwhelming sense of God's forgiveness and love.

Christ wants me to ask forgiveness and allow Him to work in other's lives. By the way, I have asked my sister to forgive me and I've asked my immediate family who have had to live with me to forgive me. The greatest help, however, is knowing God not only forgives me but He loves me. Praise His name! It is His life that gives me power to allow God's work to be done.

In closing, I used to be a person who thought winning was all important. I played sports to win, I lived my Christian life to be a winner. But I lost. All my efforts could not make me a winner.

I have found that "losing is winning since it turned me around." I thank Jesus for all the pain and all the suffering because I have found something that is worth it all. I have found Christ's life, joy and peace and that is worth losing for.

Testimony of John Best

Groundwork for Brokenness

I had been experiencing a lot of pressure and frustration in my life a number of years ago. I was angry because I thought my goals in my work were being blocked by other people. My schedule was getting busier and I was becoming increasingly tired. Although I was in Christian work as a seminary professor, I was "running out of gas" in my life.

I went to my wife with my problems but she was in so much physical pain from a back injury that she told me, "John, I'd like to give you some comfort and understanding, but I am in too much pain. I just cannot take any more of your pouring out your tales of woe." This left me feeling stranded because I had become emotionally overly-dependent upon my wife.

Through this pressure and frustration God was removing the "crutches" upon which I had been leaning. He was using the problems that I was experiencing to give me a desire for a closer walk with God.

The Process of Brokenness

For several miserable months that desire seemed unfulfilled because I was primarily viewing a closer relationship with God as a way to get Him to "fix the fix" I was in. Although I increased my Bible study and prayer I was not experiencing the peace and power that the Bible said I could have in my life. I became more troubled within and weaker and weaker.

Finally, I asked God to show me what the problem was. It was early one morning that I opened myself up for the Holy Spirit to show me anything that was not right in my life. He did.

God showed me that I had bitterness toward several people who had put me under pressure and that I needed to forgive them. I did. I forgave them one by one.

He showed me that I was sinking in a pit of self-pity and that the despair would increase as long as I continued to be self absorbed. God convinced me that trusting Him regardless of my circumstances was the only way out of my pit of self-pity.

The Lord next faced me with the issue of His Lordship in my life. Would I let Him do with me whatever He wanted? I really "sweated out" this one for awhile since up until this time I had some rigid ideas of what I would let Him do to me. Finally, I chose to entrust myself entirely to Him.

God was bringing me to a place of brokenness before Him. As I was humbled and teachable, I knew that the power for the Christian life had to come from God and not from myself, not my talents, training or personal strengths. This is something I had intellectually acknowledged before but had not personally appropriated. I had not turned from my fleshly reliance on my own resources.

In Christ and Christ in Me

The day after the Lord brought me to this place of teachableness, some friends gave me *Handbook to Happiness* by Charles Solomon. This book pointed me to the teaching of Scripture that when He brings us to salvation, God does far more than just forgive us of our sins and promise us a home in heaven. He takes us out of spiritual death in Adam and puts us into Christ's life. He exchanges our identity as sinners in Adam for a new identity as new creation saints in Christ. We are placed in Christ and Christ is placed in us. Christ wants to be our resource for life because He came into us to express His life through us (Galatians 2:20; Philippians 1:21).

God convicted me that Christ being my functional resource for life had not been happening because I had been living according to the flesh. That is, I had been trying to run my life my way and trying to get my needs met in my own resources or in others' rather than in Christ. The Lord brought me to the place where I gave up on my flesh and turned from it. I personally trusted in what the Bible says about our union with Christ in His death and burial to the power of sin. I depended upon my union with Christ in His resurrection and ascension to walk in His victory (Romans 6:1-14). As I continued to appropriate His life rather than relying on myself, Christ gave me the peace, power and deeper walk with Him that had eluded me before.

How God Spells Relief

Some of the specific patterns of flesh that the Lord gave me victory over were the fear of rejection and the fear of man. Up until this time, I had not fully relied on God's love for me and had depended too much on human love. I tried to win this acceptance on the basis of my performance or what the Bible would call "works." I feared people rejecting me. The Lord now taught me to accept the acceptance He had provided for me in Christ (Romans 15:7; John 17:23). I am totally accepted and loved by God apart from any work that I might do because I am in Christ. He is my acceptance. Therefore I don't have to let others control me by my fearing their rejection.

Another symptom that God dealt with was my fear of man (Proverbs 29:25). I feared what people would say about me or might do to me. This brought me under bondage to their control rather than being under Christ's control. But now that I know that Christ is my strength as He lives His life within me (Philippians 4:13), I don't have to fear other people.

Can you imagine the stress that these fears and performance based acceptance put on me? It was such a relief to find release from this stress in Christ! God spells relief, J E S U S.

Other results that relying on my union with Christ brought were:

1. Freedom from inferior feelings through knowing who I am in Christ.

2. Drawing close to God as an intimate friend, rather than a distant, formal, unfeeling deity.

3. Learning to cast my burdens on the Lord rather than carrying them myself.

A "Secret" Too Good to Keep Changes in Me at Dallas Theological Seminary

My fear of man particularly gripped me in relationship to my work at the seminary. Every day there I was surrounded by many other professors who were more highly trained, more intelligent and more articulate than I.

When the Lord set me free from this fear of men, I found that I could go to classes, even at the doctoral level where several of my faculty colleagues were present, and teach in freedom, not fearing what they thought of me and my performance.

Another result of my relying on my union with Christ was how I related to my students. Along with the freedom that I experienced with my peers, I now had a more genuine love for my students. My concern now was not how I was "coming across" but how they had deeper needs than learning Greek grammar. I would often take the first portion of a class to share with them the identification with Christ truths, telling them what this relationship with Him meant to me personally. I had overhead transparencies of the "Wheel and Line" diagrams from the **Handbook to Happiness** and would explain them a few at a time.

Students started coming to my office to talk about personal matters. It was so meaningful to talk on this level with them, rather than what had been typical before then: inquiries about homework, questions about a grade or other matters that were purely academic.

Establishing Exchanged Life Ministries Texas

Another significant result of experiencing Christ as my life was my desire to share Him with others. This led to my being trained in an Exchanged Life Workshop and Advanced Training and then establishing Exchanged Life Ministries Texas (now called Operation 220) in the Dallas area. Here we could minister Christ and His sufficiency to people through discipleship, conferences and training.

What a thrill it is to see people's lives transformed by Christ! The stories found in this book are only a small portion of the many who have found life in Christ through Exchanged Life Ministries. I wish you could personally meet these people. Several Christ-centered offices in Texas have been established by our training program. Hundreds are sharing Christ as life in other ways.

A Deepened Ministry

I have now turned over the leading of the office to others. I am now able to do what I love to do the most in ministry; I am researching the truths in the Bible of our union with Christ, writing books on this and presenting my teaching on many recordings as well. As God gives me health, it is my delightful honor and privilege to visit other offices that are like-minded to encourage them, lend my support, and teach them what I have learned from the Lord. Read more about my publications and consulting with other offices at www.AbundantLivingResources.org.

Resting in the Faithful One

The more Satan has attacked Carolyn and me, the more it has driven us into our only safe shelter, the Lord Jesus Christ. God has used the trials brought to us to draw us closer to Him and to cause our faith to mature and our hope to be even more stable (James 1:2-4, Romans 5:3-5).

One of the most significant things that God has done is given me a deepened and renewed trust in Christ's adequacy to be truly responsible for me and all related to me. This is in stark contrast to the weight of responsibility that I have often felt. My flesh tends to take everything (almost) very seriously.

God, in His great love for me, has wanted to relieve me of this pressure so I could be a testimony of His faithfulness, not mine. In order to do this, God let it get really "hot in the kitchen" to show me that all my well-intended great sense of responsibility was inadequate and unnecessary. First, a couple of situations developed with my children that were crushing. No matter how hard I tried or how deeply I cried, the situations didn't get better, they got worse. I was put in a position of having to either release the problems to the Lord or continue to lose sleep, have an over-taxed mind and a churned-up stomach.

Another matter that the Lord brought to the surface was my concern over finances in our family and in the ministry. I was not sure what to do about it. In fact, it seemed that little could be done to change it. Here again, the Lord stepped in with a solution I was not expecting. God is full of surprises! What all this is showing me is that its a waste of my time and energy to get worked up over anything. My life and all connected to it is in Christ's very capable hands. Why not just rest in His love, power and provision? The story of Hudson Taylor, founder of the China Inland Mission, in a booklet, *The Exchanged Life*, has joyfully refreshed me that all I need is in *Christ*. My concern, if there is any, should be preoccupation with Him, not my own condition, not my problems, not my victory or lack of it. When Taylor saw this the weight and strain was gone, though responsibilities had grown and grown for him, as they have for me.

I see, like J. Hudson Taylor did, that it is futile to find strength, intelligence or even enough faith to meet them all. It is not striving for more faith but resting in the Faithful One

The Lord is burning into my mind two things about the sufficiency of Christ:

1. *Christ* within is all I need for my needs and my identity. I need search nowhere else or in nobody else! I have been learning very vividly that God loves me unconditionally no matter what. Yet there is more. Christ should be my focus, not my getting my love need met! The love need will be met as a necessary consequence but the focus should not be there! Identity is found through what He has made me to be, yet the big thing is Christ, not my identity, even as it's in Him.

2. But that is not all! *Christ* is all I need for victory over sin and circumstances. My identity with Him in co-crucifixion renders me dead to sin (Romans 6:6, 11). My identity with Him in co- resurrection and ascension renders me more than a conqueror over circumstances (Romans 8:35-37).

I want to never see myself as apart from Christ. Since He is my rest and resource, the flesh and Satan want me not to be trusting in my union with Him. If I abide in the fact of my union with my exalted Lord, whatever does not ruffle or agitate Him today does *not* have the power to ruffle or agitate me. If it does, it's only my feelings. I don't have to let them twist me around! I can stand firm on truth, not just abstract truth, but personal truth, on Him who is the Truth that sets us free (John 8:32, 36).

BIBLIOGRAPHY
By John E. Best, Th.D.

Although I have not given details in my opinions here, you can find these features in the extensive Annotated Bibliography in my book *The Cross of Christ: The Center of Scripture, Your Life and Ministry*.[75] I have, in a few instances here, included my summaries and opinions to let you know what the longer treatment in the above book is like.

Not every possible book is included. Reading and evaluating them all is a task for which I do not have enough years left. It is also beyond the scope of this book. The ones I have included are the best up to this point but that is my opinion. I thank God that in the quarter century that I have known the full meaning of the cross there has been a great increase in the books on the exchanged life, so much so that I can not keep up with reading and critiquing them all.

---

75 John E. Best, *The Cross of Christ: The Center of Scripture, Your Life and Ministry* (Garland, TX: Abundant Living Resources, 2007). www.AbundantLivingResources.org.

General Books on the Exchanged Life

Though not a comprehensive list, I have included below the books I consider to be the most basic and helpful on the core message of our union with Christ in the cross and how He lives His life through us. *After the first listing I will have a limited list of helpful books on particular approaches to the exchanged life.*

Best, John, *Who Cares Who I Am? Who Cares What My Needs and Problems Are?* Garland, TX: Abundant Living Resources 2007, Pp. 38. www.AbundantLivingResources.org.

Edwards, Gene, *Exquisite Agony*. Jacksonville, FL: The Seed Sowers Christian Books Publishing House, 1994. Pp. 115.

Edwards, Gene, *The Highest Life*. Auburn, ME: The Seed Sowers Christian Books Publishing House, 1989. Pp. 189.

Edwards, Gene, *The Secret to the Christian Life*. Auburn, ME: The Seed Sowers Christian Books Publishing House, 1991. Pp. 148.

Evans, Tony, *Free at Last*. Chicago, IL: Moody Press, 2001. Pp. 209.

Fromke, DeVern F., *The Ultimate Intention*. Indianapolis, IN: Sure Foundation, 1998. Pp. 239.

This is a panoramic unfolding of God's ultimate intention for Himself as seen from eternity to eternity. The author contrasts the imperative necessity of seeing all things from God's eternal viewpoint, versus man's selfish attempt to use God to solve his predicaments regardless of how they fit into God's eternal purpose. He lovingly encourages the reader to pause from looking at what man can get from God and look at what God has planned as His ultimate intention for Himself, His Son, and His Holy Spirit.

De Vern Fromke, in my opinion, was one of the great Bible teachers of the twentieth century. This book strongly reflects his teaching gift in that it is filled with blackboard type diagrams and charts. This is one of the things that sets this book apart from others.

If you want thorough teaching on our union with Christ, if you want to understand the Heavenly Father's "Ultimate Intention," then this book is certainly for you because it will not only deal with the basics but also with many other over arching issues in God's divine plan. This author definitely shows that intimacy with Him is the thing closest to God's heart and that the cross is central to bringing that about.

I have been especially helped by the first few chapters, and then some of the succeeding chapters, for instance, "What the Cross Realizes for God." There are also insightful comparisons and contrasts between the *Work* of the Cross and the *Way* of the Cross.

My good friend, Bill Mallon, has done a wonderful job in revising and updating this edition (1998) and he has added many helpful questions and insights in the study guide at the end.

The many strengths of this book vastly overshadow any weaknesses that might be mentioned. I suppose the book might have a weakness for some who would not want as much detail as this book has. However, it was not written for those wanting a superficial understanding of God's purposes and work in our lives to accomplish them. I personally don't think that anybody who is serious about his or her walk of faith with Christ as life should bypass this crucial book.

Gillham, Bill, *Lifetime Guarantee*. Eugene, OR: Harvest House Publishers, 1993. Pp. 247.

Gillham, Bill, *What God Wishes Christians Knew about Christianity*. Eugene, OR: Harvest House Publishers, 1998. Pp. 283.

Needham, David, *Birthright*. Sisters, OR: Multnomah Publishers, Inc., 1999. Pp. 304.

In a sequel to his 1979 book, *Birthright,* Professor Needham examines what happened to us at the new birth, what the real meaning of regeneration is. He explains that more than simply providing forgiveness, the new birth means that we have been made new persons and that Jesus lives in us as our life. Needham disputes the view that Christians are "still sinners–just forgiven" and shows that the Scriptures teach that we are righteous saints in Christ.

He emphasizes the implications of our new birth for daily living and argues (primarily from 1 John) that God's intention for us is to live without sin–not perfectly, but consistently–and how He has provided for that through Christ. The author teaches that we do not have to continue striving to become spiritual, but that we already are spiritual in Christ. He portrays the Christian's life as one of joyous, enthusiastic victory.

This book and Professor Needham's former book, also called *Birthright,* are the best books written since the time of Martyn Lloyd-Jones on the radical change that the new birth has brought at the deepest level of our personhood. It is well documented with frequent citations from books, journals, etc. Needham argues perhaps more persuasively than any other twentieth century writer (including Lloyd-Jones), that believers have one new identity, not both an old nature and a new nature. This radical change took place in us at the cross and in our resurrection with Christ.

In spite of the excellent documentation, do not expect this book to be dry and unrelated to your personal life. On the contrary, it is an exciting book that will challenge you to rethink some of your presuppositions and patterns of living, especially your reaction to temptation and the problems of life. For some, Needham may go too far in his assertions from 1 John, that God's intention is for believers to not sin. Some will conclude that he is propounding sinless perfection, which he soundly disputes while maintaining that there is far more practical holiness for us to experience than most of us do.

While arguing his points with firm conviction, Needham couches his perspectives in such humility and kindness that no one could accuse him of being contentious. His positions may at times provoke emotional disagreement, but if these initial reactions are put aside, in the end much will be gained by fresh insights and some very practical exhortations and applications.

In my judgment one weakness in this book is that some of Needham's opinions in the first chapter about the image of God and the fall of man are debatable. Do not let these deter you from continuing on in this excellent book. Another weakness of this reissue of **Alive for the First Time** (same publisher, 1995) is that the Scripture index in that edition has been dropped in this one.

Rackets, Sally, *New Life in Christ*. Snoqualmie, WA: The Masters Touch, 1997. Pp. 28, also available in Spanish, ***Nueva Vida en Cristo***.

Smith, Hannah Whitall, *The Christian's Secret of a Happy Life*. New Kensington, PA: Whitaker House, 1983. Pp. 240.

Solomon, Charles, *The Handbook to Happiness.* Carol Stream, IL: Tyndale House Publishers, Inc., 1971, Revised, 1999. Pp. 147.

Solomon, Charles, *The Ins and Out of Rejection.* Sevierville, TN: Solomon Publications, 1991. Pp. 226.

Stone, Dan, and Smith, Greg, *The Rest of the Gospel.* Dallas, TX: One Press, 2000. Pp. 258.

Thomas, Ian, *The Saving Life of Christ and the Mystery of Godliness.* Grand Rapids, MI: Zondervan Publishing House, 1988. Pp. 288.

Trumbull, Charles G., *Victory in Christ.* Fort Washington, PA: Christian Literature Crusade, 1959. Pp. 112.

Interactive and Group Studies of the Exchanged Life

All of these exciting books have **two valuable features**: they have the material broken down into units that can easily be studied in one setting or between classes. They also ask many questions to provide you or your group with valuable interaction concerning the concepts.

Brittin, Scott D. and Grecue, Barry, *The Grace Life Handbook.* Marietta, GA: Grace Ministries International, 1994. Pp. v. + 204.

Gillham, Bill and Anabel, *The Life.* Ft. Worth, TX: Lifetime Guarantee Ministries, Inc., 1996. 11 video sessions on VHS or DVD and Study Guide. Pp. 62.

Grainger, Johnie and Patterson, Donna, *The Exchanged Life: an Invitation to Triumphant Living.* San Antonio, TX: Rhyme and Reason Word Design Studio, 2002. Pp. 103.

Rackets, Sally, *Abiding in Jesus: a Study of Our Union with Christ, Part 1.* Snoqualmie, WA: The Master's Touch, 2003. Pp. vii + 120.

Roberts, Renee, *Be Transformed: Discovering Biblical Solutions to Life's Problems.* Oklahoma City, OK: Scope Ministries International, 1998. Pp. vvi + ca. 300.

Turner, Lee C., *Grace Discipleship Course.* Sun City, AZ: Grace Discipleship Ministries Publisher, 1992. Pp. 173.

The Grace Discipleship Course is a well explained and humorously illustrated study that makes learning both fun and worthwhile. It uses the diagrams found in Charles Solomon's books and earlier presentations of the Exchanged Life Conference. It is great for groups of people just beginning to learn of their union with Christ, as we found with two groups at ELMT. There is a leader's guide and an advanced sequel as well.

Devotional Books on the Exchanged Life

Hunt, June, *Seeing Yourself Through God's Eyes: A Devotional Guide.* Dallas, TX: Hope for the Heart, 1989. Pp. 92.

Murray, Andrew, *Abide in Christ: Thoughts on the Blessed Life of Fellowship with the Son of God.* St. Louis, MO: Bible Memory Association International, n.d. Pp. 222.

Myers, Ruth and Myers, Warren, *31 Days of Praise: Enjoying God Anew.* Sisters, OR: Multnomah Publishers, Inc., 1994. Pp.157.

Many Christians are like me. They need some structure in order to guide them during times when they are not particularly stirred emotionally toward prayer and other devotional matters. This book is excellent for this type of person. It has a different topic for each day of the month and is basically a rewording of Scripture itself into personalized praise. The Myers have been good enough to give us the Scripture references and also at times give us room on the pages where we can add our own thoughts and comments.

There is no question that these people are committed to the truths of the exchanged life. Even though you will not find the typical exchanged life type words in every day of praise they occur often enough that we are reminded that they are the basis of our whole relationship to God. In addition, at the back of the book they have a helpful section on "Praise can help you experience Christ as your life." (pp. 126-136). This is an excellent addition to this book and reveals the Myers' own walk abiding in their union with Christ.

Of the hundreds of books which I cherish, this is my most commonly used book! Almost every morning I use it as a guide to some of my prayer life or use the book described immediately below. I recommend it without reservation.

Myers, Ruth and Myers, Warren, *31 Days of Power: Learning to Live in Spiritual Victory.* Sisters, OR: Multnomah Publishers, Inc., 2003. Pp. 158.

Biographies

The following books have stories of people who have appropriated Christ as life. Although many books on the exchanged life have people's stories within them, I have only included in this list the books that are devoted to biographies.

Best, John, *Exchanged Lives.* Garland, TX: Abundant Living Resources 2002, Pp. 86 plus subject index. www.AbundantLivingResources.org.

Edman, V. Raymond, *They Found the Secret.* Grand Rapids, MI: Zondervan Publishing House, 1960. Pp. 192.

Taylor, Dr. and Mrs. Howard, *Hudson Taylor's Spiritual Secret*. Chicago, IL: Moody Press, 1989. Pp. 256.

This is a history of the exploits of the pioneer missionary to inland China, J. Hudson Taylor. The book should be read with the understanding that it is a history. The title of the book mainly applies to chapter 14 in which Hudson Taylor is writing of his experiences of Christian life to his sister, which is entitled "The Exchanged Life." By the preceding statement I do mean that the exchanged life or as the authors call it "Hudson Taylor's Spiritual Secret" is not found elsewhere in the book. What I do mean though is that if you want Hudson Taylor's spiritual secret all gathered in one compact form, chapter 14 is for you.

The book is high adventure as far as missionary biographies go, so read it with the idea that you're going to find the story of a courageous, faithful and steadfast pioneer in the modern missionary movement. Christ within enabled him to endure and be effective in the midst of tremendous difficulties.

Some have speculated that Hudson Taylor was the one who originated the term "the exchanged life." This may be so, but these types of things are hard to actually determine with historical certainty.

Highly recommended reading.

Bible Expositions

The following books emphasize the truths of the exchanged life as they expound upon extended passages of Scripture, truths that are not arranged topically but according to the biblical text.

I have only included in the main list the ones I have read entirely, thus it is short. Usually I use expositions of Scripture for their comments here and there on passages and do not read these from cover to cover.

In addition to the main books at the end of this list, I am first listing other authors who have several expositions of Bible books and have some comments based on the message of our union with Christ. However, I have not read their books entirely, so I cannot vouch that the message is upheld consistently. Some of those authors are (in alphabetical order):

Barnhouse, Donald Grey. A multivolume set on Romans.

Chambers, Oswald. Go to *The Complete Works of Oswald Chambers* (Grand Rapids, MI: Discovery House Publishers, 2000) for all of the below or in some cases individual books can be found, as noted: *Gems from Genesis; Baffled to Fight Better,* on Job; *The Shade of His Hand*, on Ecclesiastes; (Partial) Notes on

Isaiah, Jeremiah, and Ezekiel, never published as separate books; and *Studies in the Sermon on the Mount*, on Matthew 5–7.

Darby, John Nelson. Commentaries on many books of the Bible.

Hodges, Zane. Free grace-oriented expositions of James, the General Epistles, and the Epistles of John.

Kuydendall, David. An exposition of Romans 5:12–8:39 called *Here's Life*.

Lloyd-Jones, D. Martyn. Three books of exposition on Romans 6–8.

McIntosh, C. H. (C.H.M.). Scholarly, devotional and readable *Notes on the Pentateuch*, the first five books of the Bible.

Murray, Andrew. Devotional treatment of Hebrews and perhaps other books of the Bible.

Newell, William R. Romans and Hebrews "verse by verse."

Stedman, Ray. Expositions of Romans, Hebrews and other Bible books.

Keep in mind that since the exchanged life is based on the plain truth of Scripture, many helpful insights can be gained in other commentaries as well. Some are also very good at resolving problems in the Bible. So don't hesitate to consult commentaries that are careful with the text, interpret it literally and are Christ honoring. Hundreds of expositions would fit into this category.

You will find in passages that specifically deal with the exchanged life (Romans 6—8 for instance) that the literal interpreters will be pretty clear.

Do be careful of the ever present danger of legalism: that is, God blesses us because of our obedience rather than grace: God blesses us and because of this we obey by His life within.

Now for a short list of expositions that I have read (or written) entirely and that are consistent in sharing the message of the exchanged life.

Main List

Best, John E., *Romans 6—8 Study Notes*. Garland, TX: Abundant Living Resources, 2007. Pp. 101. www.AbundantLivingResources.org.

Best, John E., *Romans 8:1-17, God's Spirit in You for Power and Intimacy*. Garland, TX: Abundant Living Resources, 2007. Pp. 44. www.AbundantLivingResources.org.

Flaten, Dick. *The Marvelous Exchange*. Dallas, TX: Exchanged Life Ministries Texas, 1999. Pp. i-xviii, 101.

The subtitles to this book tell a lot. "Discerning the Power of Spiritual Union with Christ," "An Exposition of Romans 6:1-14." This book is very needed because in it Pastor Flaten "presents the key to triumphant Christian living: knowing and counting on what God has already accomplished at the cross of Christ… what He did [there] in us because of our spiritual union with Him in His death and resurrection" (from the back cover and page xii).

The author's treatment of these crucial truths from this vital passage is warm, clear and helpful. He wrote with the tone of a loving pastor, which he was for almost 20 years.

Pastor Flaten wisely chose the New American Standard Bible (as I also have) for the careful exposition that he wanted to do. At the end of several sections he composed enlightening "summary paraphrases" which are freer than the NASB and allow him to weave into the text his explanatory thoughts.

He has many beneficial quotations which are especially good from John Murray, Martyn Lloyd-Jones and David Needham, all of which have done extensive work in Romans six from an identity in union with Christ perspective.

These and many other things are the strengths of this work. The only weakness, in my opinion, is Flaten's avoidance of the mention of the word "spirit" in relationship to our new identity in Christ. This is especially notable in his treatment of Romans 6:2-7 and 11 which I don't think can be clearly and consistently understood without knowing that it is our spirit being spoken of. Dick told me that he avoided the word because he wanted the message of the book to reach those who do not hold to the spirit, soul, body distinctions. Nevertheless he did see these distinctions himself and often uses the word "spiritual," as in "spiritual union" (see the subtitle and many other places), "spiritual birth" and "spiritual identity" (often).

The book ends strongly with three very useful appendices; "Living in Dependence upon God," "Old Man vs. New Man," and "Freedom from the Law."

I had the honor of knowing Dick Flaten well as a friend and fellow staff member at Exchanged Life Ministries Texas. He lived out of his spiritual union with Christ in his everyday life even as cancer slowly took his physical life from him. It is no surprise to me that, with the able assistance of Greg Smith, he produced this exposition that is warm, clear and helpful.

CITED AUTHORS

This is for the body of the book and does not include the Bibliography.

Author

William Barclay
John E. Best
John Broadus
Donald K. Campbell
Lewis Sperry Chafer
G. K. Chesterton
Alfred Edersheim
Richard Flaten
Bob George
Bill Gillham
Alice Gray
Everett F. Harrison
John Peter Lange
Jamie Lash
Lee LeFebre
R. C. H. Lenski
C. S. Lewis
Martyn Lloyd-Jones
Charles McCall

Steve McVey
Leon Morris
David Needham
J. Dwight Pentecost
Archibald T. Robertson
Ray Rodgers
Charles Caldwell Ryrie
W. Graham Scroggie
Greg Smith
Hannah Whitall Smith
John Souter
Dan Stone
W. E. Vine
Mark and Ruth Virkler
John F. Walvoord
Tom Weaver
Roy B. Zuck

Made in the USA
Columbia, SC
29 October 2024